I Am Izzu
and
Chuck is on a Quest

Level 3 – Yellow

Helpful Hints for Reading at Home

The graphemes (written letters) and phonemes (units of sound) used throughout this series are aligned with Letters and Sounds. This offers a consistent approach to learning whether reading at home or in the classroom.

HERE IS A LIST OF ALTERNATIVE PHONEMES FOR THIS PHASE OF LEARNING. AN EXAMPLE OF THE PRONUNCIATION CAN BE FOUND IN BRACKETS.

Phase 3			
j (jug)	v (van)	w (wet)	x (fox)
y (yellow)	z (zoo)	zz (buzz)	qu (quick)
ch (chip)	sh (shop)	th (thin/then)	ng (ring)
ai (rain)	ee (feet)	igh (night)	oa (boat)
oo (boot/look)	ar (farm)	or (for)	ur (hurt)
ow (cow)	oi (coin)	ear (dear)	air (fair)
ure (sure)	er (corner)		

HERE ARE SOME WORDS WHICH YOUR CHILD MAY FIND TRICKY.

Phase 3 Tricky Words			
he	you	she	they
we	all	me	are
be	my	was	her

TOP TIPS FOR HELPING YOUR CHILD TO READ:

• Allow children time to break down unfamiliar words into units of sound and then encourage children to string these sounds together to create the word.

• Encourage your child to point out any focus phonics when they are used.

• Read through the book more than once to grow confidence.

• Ask simple questions about the text to assess understanding.

• Encourage children to use illustrations as prompts.

This book focuses on the phonemes /zz/ and /qu/ and is a yellow level 3 book band.

I Am Izza
and
Chuck is on a Quest

Written by
Kirsty Holmes
& Robin Twiddy

Illustrated by
Lynne Feng
& Amy Li

Can you say this sound and draw it with your finger?

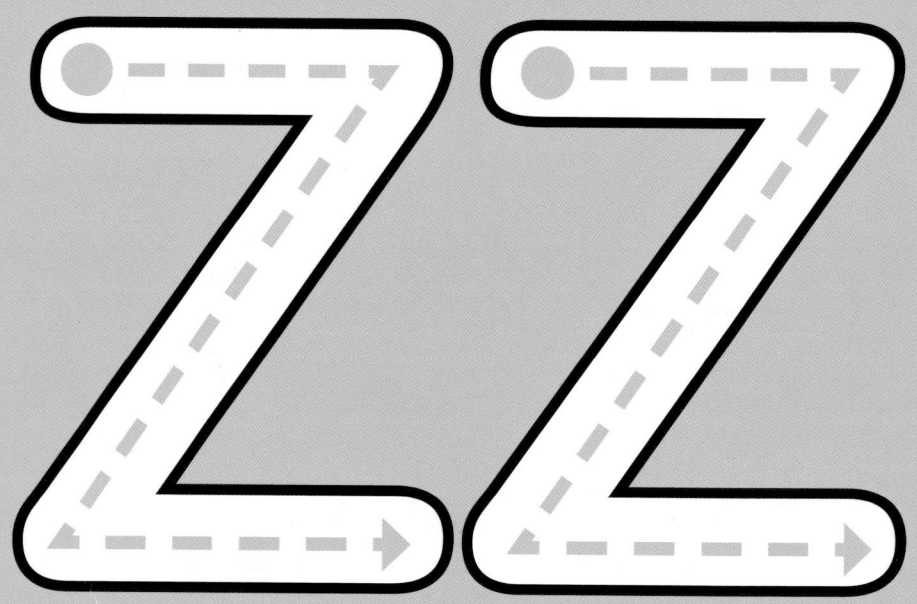

I Am Izza

Written by
Kirsty Holmes

Illustrated by
Lynne Feng

Izza meets an ox.

The ox is big.

Izza meets a fox.

The fox is red.

Izza meets a buzzing bee. Buzz! Buzz!

The bee zigs and zags.

Izza meets a boxer dog.

The boxer dog wags his tail.

Izza meets a zebra.

The zebra is not pink.

Izza is not an ox, a fox, a bee, a dog or a zebra.

Izza is pink. Izza has fuzz.

Can you say this sound and draw it with your finger?

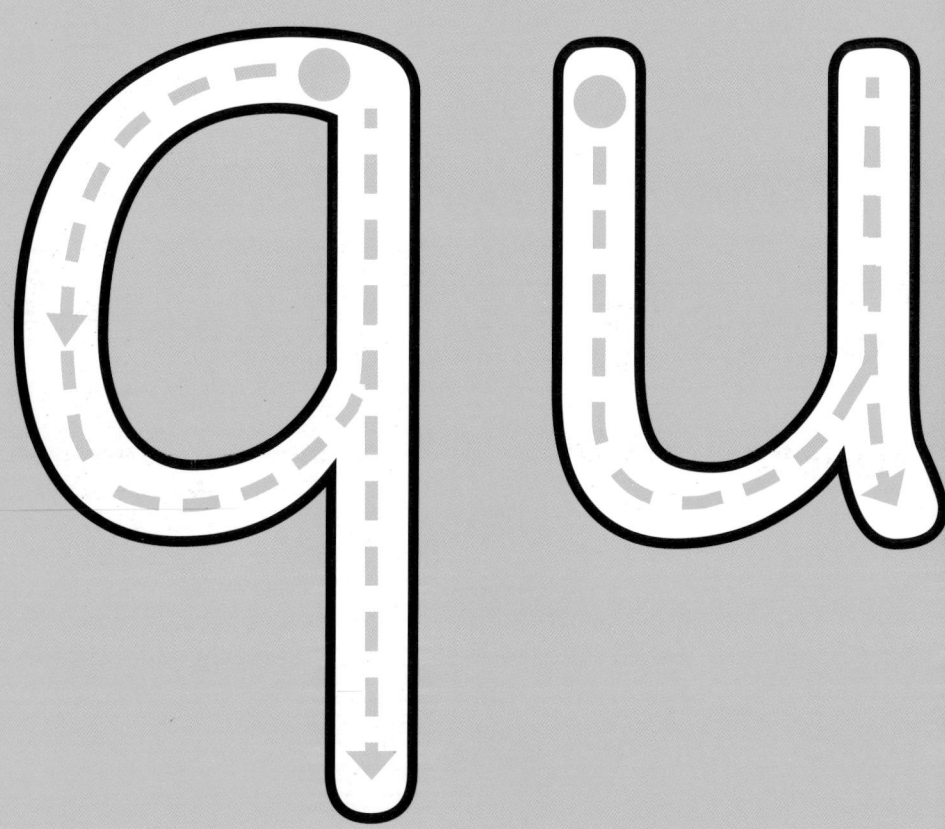

Chuck Is on a Quest

Written by
Robin Twiddy

Illustrated by
Amy Li

Chuck is on a quest. Chuck needs to go to the den.

Look! The pond of pongs and shells.

Chuck is on the hill of the chill chimps.

It is a big quest. Chuck will not quit.

Up the hill of big chins. Chuck cannot quit.

Shush, Chuck! This is the hall of naps.

Chuck is on a quest, but he will not quit.

Chuck is on a path. Look at the men.

It is the den. Chuck needs to hit the duck to get in.

The den is full of cash.

Be quick, Chuck. Get all of the cash.

It is the end of the quest. Chuck needs to go back. It will not be quick!

©2021 **BookLife Publishing Ltd.**
King's Lynn, Norfolk PE30 4LS

ISBN 978-1-83927-876-1

All rights reserved. Printed in Malta.
A catalogue record for this book is available from the British Library.
I Am Izza
Written by Kirsty Holmes
Illustrated by Lynne Feng

Chuck Is on a Quest
Written by Robin Twiddy
Illustrated by Amy Li

An Introduction to BookLife Readers...

Our Readers have been specifically created in line with the London Institute of Education's approach to book banding and are phonetically decodable and ordered to support each phase of the Letters and Sounds document.

Each book has been created to provide the best possible reading and learning experience. Our aim is to share our love of books with children, providing both emerging readers and prolific page-turners with beautiful books that are guaranteed to provoke interest and learning, regardless of ability.

BOOK BAND GRADED using the Institute of Education's approach to levelling.

PHONETICALLY DECODABLE supporting each phase of Letters and Sounds.

EXERCISES AND QUESTIONS to offer reinforcement and to ascertain comprehension.

BEAUTIFULLY ILLUSTRATED to inspire and provoke engagement, providing a variety of styles for the reader to enjoy whilst reading through the series.

AUTHOR INSIGHT:
ROBIN TWIDDY

Robin Twiddy possesses a Cambridge-based first class honours degree in psychosocial studies. He also has a certificate in Teaching in the Lifelong Sector, and a post graduate certificate in Consumer Psychology. A father of two, Robin has written over 70 titles for BookLife.

KIRSTY HOLMES

Kirsty Holmes, holder of a BA, PGCE, and an MA, was born in Norfolk, England. She has written over 60 books for BookLife Publishing, and her stories are full of imagination, creativity and fun.

This book focuses on the phonemes /zz/ and /qu/ and is a yellow level 3 book band.

Additional images courtesy of Shutterstock.com.
Chuck is on a Quest p20–21 – Alfmaler, p22–23 Kriengsuk Prasroetsung, p28–29 – peiyang, HappyPictures, p30–31 – peiyang, HappyPictures